" Jen Calleja's furious long poem expresses a great passion for life in its unembellished, unruly form, which includes and incorporates failure, imperfection and even death. A great reminder that we do not need to wait until everything is alright – dust turns out to be a precondition for jest, tenderness and beauty. "

Marion Poschmann

author of *The Pine Islands*

" In this beautiful book, Jen Calleja conjures desire and loss, depth and wistfulness, through her signature hypnotic melodies. We see her plucked blackberries, her antique photos, her infant gulls, and we recognise the pained loss of "sunset/on the toilet paper". Longings dwell here, as wondrous and abundant as dust. "

Doireann Ní Ghríofa

author of *A Ghost in the Throat*

Dust Sucker

Design and illustration by Patrick Fisher of Frontwards Design
Photograph of Jen Calleja by Robin Christian
Photograph of Carolina Schutti by Simon Rainer

ISBN: 978-1-7396160-0-7

First published in the UK in 2023 by Makina Books · makinabooks.com

Printed in the UK by Henry Ling Limited, at the Dorset Press, Dorchester

'Dust Sucker' previously published in *The White Review*

The writing and the translation of this work has been funded by the Federal Ministry for European and International Affairs of Austria as part of the "Internationale Literaturdialoge 2021" project.

= Federal Ministry
Republic of Austria
European and International
Affairs

Dust Sucker

your eyes might be open; they might be closed

Jen Calleja

Dustsceawung *(Old English): contemplation of the fact that dust used to be other things – the walls of a city, the chief of the guards, a book, a great tree: dust is always the ultimate destination. Such contemplation may loosen the grip of our worldly desires.*

—'Untranslatable Words',
   The School of Life, 2018

my living is thick and filthy

I start the day by reading obituaries
like I'm smoking a morning cigarette,
ash in my one eye, the other tucked under my pillow

this is the crap I breathe to dust absurdity
over everything

I saw this coming in my periphery
I'm short-sighted, so never wear
my glasses

I'm a painter brushing a wash for the background,
everything atomised
beyond a point

❖

making coffee, drinking water at the sink,
an evening with dear friends:
the warm up frames in the comic strip,
the montage of my trivial activities before
the incident

the creak on the stairs in the new house
is a home invasion

the click of the boiler, like someone striking a match,
foreshadows a gas explosion

well *someone* is going to stop breathing

✻

the german word for hoover is staubsauger, lit. dust sucker
and you may call a baby säugling – little suckler
we call them tot, resembling das deutsche wort for 'dead'
staubschauen, like the old english word for the contemplation of dust,
might be translated as 'dust-gazing'

sounds irritating on the eyes

✻

brambles tumbled over the back wall overnight
I pick the berries
bunches of black balloons
leaving the infants and the mouldy ones

grey and puffy like a bulldog's face

I make a crumble and give it to a neighbour
I think *this is living*
but my mind sees through it

there are hundreds of berries along the main road

I wouldn't touch them

juicy with fumes and roar and residue
from discarded drinks bottles
each black bubble
filled with cola and stout

❉

squatting on low stools in a pub full of lungs
we proclaimed we'd *started trying*
wet smiles, motes drifting in sunbeams

years later, no one asks anymore

that's all a load of old dust

✽

we moved away to the coast

I slide out a photobook of seaside towns in the sixties
the grandmothers getting ice-creams
the husband looking past his wife
the wife at her wedding ring
couples dancing outside the nearby pavilion

they're just a sandy beach now

✽

the roofs are heaving with seagulls
the fluffy grey babies mew, warming up their voices
for adulthood
the big ones pump out trumpet honks

gulls have piñata'd the bags of recycling
sending cans rolling down the hill like a flood

✽

my dad still manoeuvres me to walk on the inside of the pavement

warns me of hitchhikers and roadside merchants

recalls a cluster of his school friends

who floated out to sea on a raft

forever

t/here I am in my baggy swimming costume

a fiver from a charity shop

(previous owner probably eighty)

demanding through my ice-cream cone

don't swim out too far

t/here wearing inappropriate footwear

on a walk in the forest, thinking I can feel

ticks all over my body, pleading

careful not to touch it

as someone pulls aside a fern to flash

an enormous mushroom, gills inverted like a blown out umbrella

❋

look, a pony ! a woodlouse !

a cow ! a wasp ! a frog ! a dragonfly !

a newt !

a neutral word in german is baby

our friend's baby says *steam* when it sees *steam, smoke, clouds*

we play in the sandpit together until das baby suddenly remembers mama
feels baby shame

could I bear to give someone the forever-feeling of having
left the heating on?

I slide out a baby-weaning book and get fixated on the risks of eating:

Introduce common allergens, never two on the same day.

a pic of a baby's blotchy face after cashew butter,
tests reveal: also pistachios

the normality of gagging

my mum's greatest fear for us: choking

no lollipops

she has no appetite these days

she sucks ice-lollies

the baby kneels on a strawberry
pink juice on white linen

when we get home there's a sunset
on the toilet paper, and me
falling for the fib for the fortieth month
that debris a baby makes

my body feels crisp and brittle, a fire hazard
a flight risk

I am a sand castle of a woman

✲

if I breathe too much exhaust it will lodge in my lungs,
bear a grudge

I feel like I'm walking along the curb of a busy road
coughing, eyes running

I need a good thump,

like thrashing a rug after winter

*

for too long
woodland and forest alike have been seen
as the side salad to the steak
the crust on the jam/ham sandwich
somehow: the past

they were eternity all along

a zillion specks
no beginning no end
camouflage correlated
in dialogue
over millennia

*

the tread of my shoe is a display case
cradling a fragment from
my daily meandering

I have a display case of mud clots slowly crumbling

I wake in the night and calmly think: is that a blood clot
gently rumbling

❊

dusting for fingerprints
chalky white over everything
like a tick
suckling the juice, rotten little sucker!
leaving our mark
like a snail trailing over books
it didn't write

❊

cocoa on a cappuccino in the shape of a toad

the cat comes in sparkling with pollen and seeds

❊

my desk is piled high with

charcoal dust

it trickles from between book covers
into the covers of my bed

I spend my time sieving it, moving it from
one bucket to the next

*

I'd rather sleep on a beach
than in my bed

the dusty feeling on my hands afterwards
from gripping salty stones and shells
like after hoovering up a dish of pistachios

*

white plastic bags of
reasonably priced fruit   günstiges obst
wash off the rough film of pesticide

dusty scent of a peach tickling my throat

✳

when my friends know I'm leaving
they start hoovering and won't stop till I'm gone

my friends
mycelium

✳

german feels chewy and sweet on my tongue,
not flaky, not like choking-hazard english

I roll maltese around in my mouth like an everlasting gobstopper
that gets no smaller, no matter how much
I suck

my dad won't put his bil-malti teeth in anymore,
my mum mimics her irish ma only never

she keeps her name out her mouth

✳

my parents' air
fizzes and froths with laughter
in spite of everything

so why in spite of not much
are we submerged in CO_2 sighs

✤

I've got names gathering dust in a folder on my phone

you can always adopt

like adding hot water to granules
but it ain't all gravy

the website depicts adoption as a winding asphalt road
all sleeping policemen and no rousing bumps

you can always adapt

✤

I've come unshelled

envious of the slug, satisfied bohemian hermaphrodite

a.k.a nacktschnecke		naked schnecke	naked snail
like in maltese, bugharwien		naked bebbuxu	beb-bu-shoo!
bébé	boo-boo	shoesneverworn	
bambino	to	babushka	
masc.	to	fem.	
bambina, surely?		"derog. equiv. bimbo"	

✻

I'm the diplomat between my lover and my body
but no interpreters are ever at hand

when it's time for that famous intimacy
I'm always constricted in a musty latex catsuit from the eighties
and the zip is jammed

I think I can proceed but then
a flea bites me on the ankle
dust bunnies tumbleweed under the bed

the bunnies and the flea are of the opinion
that I should just close my eyes

you'll see

❃

shocked to see the head of a seal like a black balloon
we'd forgotten there were animals in the sea

look, a seal !
look, a dolphin !

yellow buoys like lint from a duster

wishy-washy sea kneading the shore, surfy hands
rolling pebbles like dice when it has
everything to lose

❃

don't say a poem can't be a to-do list or a diary or showing
my workings & findings

this is, in fact, a graph

❃

I brush down my shoulders and sleeves
shake my hair, sending out a fine cloud, like steam

I will wear my glasses every day

I will keep writing missives on smeared glass

these words have floated and alighted in this exact arrangement

this has been my vacuum cleaner

my gaze drips warmly over everything

❊

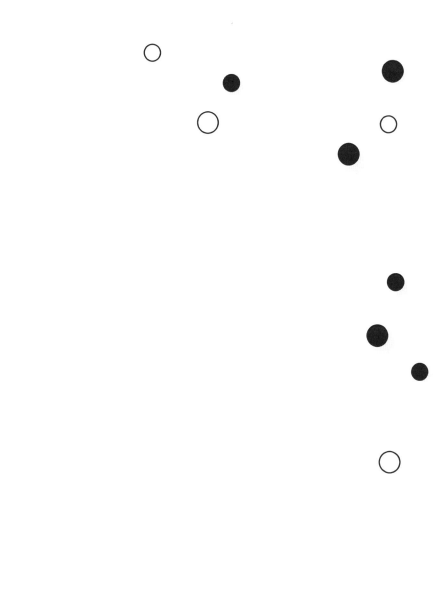

Staub-
schlucker

deine Augen
könnten offen sein
oder geschlossen

Jen Calleja

Übersetzt von
Carolina Schutti

Dustsceawung *(Altenglisch): Nachsinnen über die Tatsache, dass Staub einmal etwas anderes war – die Mauern einer Stadt, der Oberste der Wachen, ein Buch, ein großer Baum: Staub ist immer der letzte Bestimmungsort. Eine solche Betrachtung kann uns aus der Umklammerung unserer weltlichen Begierden lösen.*

—„Unübersetzbare Worte"
   Die Schule des Lebens, 2018

mein Leben ist dick und schmutzig

ich beginne den Tag mit dem Lesen von Nachrufen,
als ob ich eine Morgenzigarette rauchen würde,
Asche in meinem einen Auge, das andere ist unter meinem Kissen versteckt

das ist der Dreck, den ich atme, um Absurdität
über alles zu stäuben

ich sah das aus dem Augenwinkel kommen
bin kurzsichtig, trage daher nie
meine Brille

ich bin eine Malerin, pinsle Farbe für den Hintergrund auf,
alles zerstäubt,
was weiter entfernt ist

*

koche Kaffee, trinke Wasser an der Spüle,
verbringe einen Abend mit lieben Freunden:
die ersten Bilder des Comicstrips,
die Montage meiner belanglosen Tätigkeiten vor dem
Ereignis

das Knarren der Treppe im neuen Haus
ist ein bewaffneter Raubüberfall

das Klicken des Boilers, als zünde jemand ein Streichholz an,
ist Vorbote einer Gasexplosion

nun, *jemand* wird aufhören zu atmen

❈

das deutsche Wort für *hoover* ist Staubsauger, wörtlich gesprochen,
und man nennt ein Baby Säugling - kleiner Saugender
wir nennen sie *tot*, ähnlich dem deutschen Wort für die Toten
dustsceawung, wie das altenglische Wort für die Betrachtung von Staub,
könnte man mit ‚staub-schauen' übersetzen

klingt nach Augenreizung

❈

Brombeergestrüpp ist nachts über die hintere Mauer gestürzt
ich pflücke die Früchte
Sträuße schwarzer Luftballons
lasse die kleinen hängen und auch die verschimmelten

grau und aufgedunsen wie ein Bulldoggengesicht

ich backe Streuselkuchen und bringe ihn einem Nachbarn
ich denke, *das ist das Leben*
doch mein Verstand durchschaut das

es gibt Hunderte von Beeren entlang der Hauptstraße

ich würde sie niemals berühren

klebrig von Qualm und Getöse und Rückständen
von weggeworfenen Getränkeflaschen
jede einzelne schwarze Blase
gefüllt mit Cola und dunklem Bier

*

auf niedrigen Stühlen hockend in einem Pub voller Lungen
verkündeten wir, dass wir *es versuchen*
feuchte Lächeln, zwischen Sonnenstrahlen treibende Partikel

Jahre später fragt niemand mehr nach

das ist alles nur ein Haufen alten Staubes

✻

wir zogen weg an die Küste

ich hole ein Fotobuch mit Küstenstädten aus den Sechzigern heraus
die Großmütter bekommen Eis
der Ehemann blickt an seiner Frau vorbei
die Frau schaut auf ihren Ehering
Paare tanzen vor dem nahegelegenen Pavillon

sie sind jetzt nur noch ein Sandstrand

✻

auf den Dächern wimmelt es von Seemöwen
die flauschigen, grauen Babys fiepen, wärmen ihre Stimmen
für das Erwachsensein auf
die Großen stoßen Trompetengeschmetter aus

für die Möwen sind die Recycling-Säcke Geschenktöpfe aus Ton
sie lassen Konservendosen den Hügel hinunterrollen wie eine Flut

✻

mein Vater bringt mich immer noch dazu,
auf der Innenseite des Bürgersteigs zu gehen
warnt mich vor Anhaltern und Straßenhändlern
erinnert an eine Gruppe seiner Schulfreunde
die auf einem Floß aufs Meer hinausgetrieben sind
für immer

hier und da bin ich in meinem schlabbrigen Badeanzug
für einen Fünfer aus einem Wohlfahrtsgeschäft
(frühere Besitzerin wahrscheinlich achtzig)
fordernd durch meine Eistüte hindurch
schwimm nicht zu weit hinaus

hier und da mit unpassendem Schuhwerk
auf einem Spaziergang im Wald, ich glaube, ich kann
Zecken am ganzen Körper spüren, ich bitte darum,
vorsichtig zu sein, um ihn nicht zu berühren,
als jemand einen Farn beiseite schiebt, um
einen riesigen Pilz zu zeigen, Lamellen obenauf
wie ein herausgebrochener Regenschirm

✳

schau, ein Pony ! eine Kellerassel !
eine Kuh ! eine Wespe ! ein Frosch ! eine Libelle !
ein Molch !

ein neutrales Wort auf Deutsch ist *Baby*

das Baby unserer Freunde sagt *Dampf*, wenn es *Dampf, Rauch, Wolken* sieht

wir spielen zusammen im Sandkasten, als das Baby sich plötzlich
an Mama erinnert
Babyscham verspürt

könnte ich es ertragen, jemandem das ewige Gefühl zu geben,
die Heizung angelassen zu haben?

ich ziehe ein Buch über Säuglingsentwöhnung hervor
und fixiere mich auf die Risiken des Essens:

Häufige Allergene einführen, niemals zwei am selben Tag.

ein Bild vom fleckigen Gesicht eines Babys nach Cashewbutter,
Tests zeigen: auch Pistazien

die Normalität des Würgens

die größte Angst meiner Mutter um uns: Ersticken

keine Lutscher

sie hat keinen Appetit mehr
sie lutscht Wassereis

das Baby kniet auf einer Erdbeere
pinker Saft auf weißem Leinen

als wir nach Hause kommen, ist ein Sonnenuntergang
auf dem Toilettenpapier zu sehen, und ich
falle den vierzigsten Monat auf den Schwindel herein,
dass man aus Trümmern ein Baby machen kann

mein Körper fühlt sich brüchig und verdorrt an, Feuergefahr,
ein Fluchtrisiko

bin eine Sandburg von einer Frau

✸

wenn ich zu viele Abgase einatme, werden sie sich in meiner Lunge festsetzen,
Groll hegen

ich fühle mich, als würde ich am Bordstein einer belebten Straße entlanglaufen
hustend, mit tränenden Augen

ich brauche einen ordentlichen Schlag
als klopfte man nach dem Winter einen Teppich aus

✶

viel zu lange
wurden Wald und Forst gleichermaßen
als Beilagensalat zum Steak gesehen
die Kruste auf dem Marmeladen-Schinken-Sandwich
irgendwie: die Vergangenheit

sie waren seit jeher die Ewigkeit

eine Zillion Staubkörnchen
kein Anfang kein Ende
Camouflage gefangen
im Dialog
Jahrtausende lang

✶

das Profil meines Schuhs ist eine Vitrine,
die ein Bruchstück meines
täglichen Mäanderns wiegt

ich habe eine Vitrine mit langsam zerbröckelnden Lehmklumpen

ich erwache in der Nacht und denke ruhig: ist es ein Blutgerinnsel
das hier so sanft rumpelt

✳

zur Suche von Fingerabdrücken verteilter Staub
kreidiges Weiß über allem
wie eine Zecke,
die den Saft trinkt, mieser kleiner Sauger!
unsere Spur hinterlassend
wie eine Schnecke, über Bücher kriechend,
die sie nicht geschrieben hat

✳

Kakao auf einem Cappuccino in Form einer Kröte

die Katze kommt herein, glitzernd von Pollen und Samen

✼

mein Schreibtisch ist dick bedeckt mit
Kohlenstaub

er rieselt zwischen Buchdeckeln heraus
hinein in die Decken meines Bettes

ich verbringe meine Zeit damit, ihn zu sieben, ihn von
einem Eimer in den nächsten zu füllen

✼

ich würde lieber an einem Strand schlafen
als in meinem Bett

das staubige Gefühl an meinen Händen nach dem
Anfassen von salzigen Steinen und Muscheln
wie nach dem gierigen Verschlingen einer Schale mit Pistazien

✼

weiße Plastiktüten mit
günstigem Obst   *cheap fruit*

wasche den rauen Pestizidfilm ab
der staubige Duft eines Pfirsichs kitzelt meine Kehle

✳

wenn meine Freunde wissen, dass ich gehe,
fangen sie an staubzusaugen und hören nicht auf, bis ich weg bin

meine Freunde
Myzel

✳

das Deutsche fühlt sich auf meiner Zunge klebrig und süß an,
nicht flockig, nicht wie das Englische mit seinem hohen Erstickungsrisiko

ich rolle das Maltesische in meinem Mund herum wie einen Riesenlollipop,
der nicht kleiner wird, egal wie sehr
ich lutsche

mein Vater setzt seine bil-Malti-Zähne nicht mehr ein,
meine Mutter ahmt ihre irische Mama niemals nicht nach

sie nimmt ihren Namen nicht in den Mund

✳

die Luft meiner Eltern
sprudelt und schäumt vor Lachen
trotz allem

warum also sind wir, trotz so Wenigem,
in CO_2-Seufzern versunken?

✳

ich habe Namen, die in einem Verzeichnis auf meinem Telefon verstauben

Sie können immer adoptieren

wie die Zugabe von heißem Wasser zu Pulver
doch es ist nicht einfach nur eine Soße

die Website stellt Adoption als gewundene Asphaltstraße dar
Bodenwellen und kein Babybauch

Sie können sich jederzeit adaptieren

✳

ich bin ohne Schale gekommen

neidisch auf die Nacktschnecke, zufriedener Böhmischer Zwitter

a.k.a *slug*		nackte *snail*	nackte Schnecke
wie auf Maltesisch, bugħarwien		nackte bebbuxu	beb-bu-shoo!
bébé	boo-boo	nie-getragene-Schuhe	
bambino	to	babushka	
masc.	to	fem.	
bambina, sicher?		"derog. equiv. bimbo"	

❉

ich bin Diplomatin, vermittle zwischen meinem Liebhaber und meinem Körper,
aber es sind nie Dolmetscher zur Hand

wenn es Zeit ist für die berühmte Intimität
bin ich stets in einem muffigen Latex-Catsuit aus den Achtzigern eingeschnürt
und der Reißverschluss klemmt

ich denke, ich kann weitermachen, aber dann
beißt mich ein Floh in den Knöchel
Wollmäuse tummeln sich unter dem Bett

die Mäuse und der Floh sind der Meinung
ich sollte einfach die Augen schließen

du wirst sehen

❋

erschrocken, den Kopf einer Robbe zu erblicken wie einen schwarzen Ballon
wir hatten vergessen, dass es Tiere im Meer gibt

schau, eine Robbe !
schau, ein Delfin !

gelbe Bojen wie Fussel aus einem Staubtuch

ein verschwommenes Meer, das die Küste formt, wogende Hände,
die Kieselsteine wie Würfel rollen, wenn es alles
zu verlieren hat

❋

sag nicht, ein Gedicht kann keine To-do-Liste und kein Tagebuch sein oder
nicht meine Tätigkeiten & Erkenntisse zeigen

dies ist, in der Tat, ein Diagramm

❋

37

ich bürste meine Schultern und Ärmel ab,
schüttle mein Haar, das eine feine Wolke aussendet, wie Dampf

ich werde jeden Tag meine Brille tragen

ich werde weiterhin Mitteilungen auf verschmiertes Glas schreiben

diese Worte schwebten und landeten in exakt dieser Anordnung

dies war mein Staubsauger

mein Blick tropft warm über das alles hier

✻

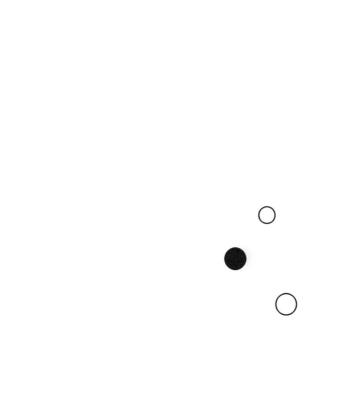

Also available from Makina Books

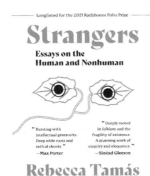

In *Strangers*, Rebecca Tamás explores where the human and nonhuman meet, and why this delicate connection just might be the most important relationship of our times. From 'On Watermelon' to 'On Grief', Tamás' essays are exhilarating to read in their radical and original exploration of the links between the environmental, the political, the folkloric and the historical.

Grief Stitches is a remarkable series of poems that exist in a continual state of suspension. Throughout, there is an uncanny sense of 'almost'—almost understanding—almost recovering from—almost suffocating—almost free. These poems crackle with vividity as much as they shift, challenging us to consider the speakers' weighted existence as they navigate between recovery and survival, charm and approval.

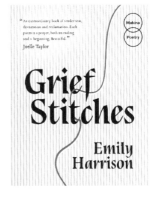

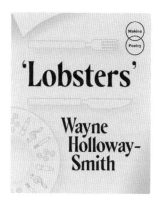

In *Lobsters*, Wayne Holloway-Smith turns his innovative poetics towards an exhilarating new work that is part songbook, part elastic melodrama. Somewhere, in between the expansive and claustrophobic, the reader is offered a new space, crammed full with the music of what life gives and withholds.

Hyperlove burns with frustration and fervour. In this incisive lyric essay, the creative mixes with the critical, as Morris looks to the mystics, to pop culture, to writing itself, dislocating categories of love and forming a radical and original exploration of desire as a woman.

About the author

Jen Calleja is the author of *Vehicle: a verse novel* (Prototype, 2023), *I'm Afraid That's All We've Got Time For* (Prototype, 2020), *Goblins* (Rough Trade Books, 2020), *Hamburger in the Archive* (if a leaf falls, 2019) and *Serious Justice* (Test Centre, 2016). She was shortlisted for the Man Booker International Prize 2019 for her translation of Marion Poschmann's *The Pine Islands* and was the inaugural Translator in Residence at the British Library. Jen is co-publisher at Praspar Press, which publishes contemporary Maltese literature in English and English translation. She lives in Hastings, UK.

About the translator

Carolina Schutti was born in Innsbruck in 1976. After completing her doctorate on Elias Canetti, she taught at the University of Florence before turning to literary writing. Her books have been awarded numerous prizes and scholarships, including the European Union Prize for Literature, and translated into eighteen languages. In early 2021, the novel *Der Himmel ist ein kleiner Kreis* was published by Droschl Literaturverlag. She was nominated for the Ingeborg Bachmann Prize with an excerpt from it.

Über die Autorin

Jen Calleja ist die Autorin von *Vehicle: a verse novel* (Prototype, 2023), *I'm Afraid That's All We've Got Time For* (Prototype, 2020), *Goblins* (Rough Trade Books, 2020), *Hamburger in the Archive* (if a leaf falls, 2019) und *Serious Justice* (Test Centre, 2016). Mit ihrer Übersetzung von Marion Poschmanns *The Pine Islands* stand sie auf der Shortlist für den Man Booker International Prize 2019 und war die erste Stipendiatin des Translator-in-Residence Programms an der British Library. Jen ist Mitherausgeberin bei Praspar Press, wo zeitgenössische maltesische Literatur in englischer Sprache und in englischer Übersetzung veröffentlicht wird. Sie lebt in Hastings, UK.

Über die Übersetzerin

Carolina Schutti wurde 1976 in Innsbruck geboren. Nach ihrer Promotion über Elias Canetti war sie zunächst Lektorin an der Universität Florenz, ehe sie sich dem literarischen Schreiben zuwandte. Ihre Bücher wurden mit zahlreichen Preisen und Stipendien ausgezeichnet, u.a. mit dem European Union Prize for Literature, sowie in achtzehn Sprachen übersetzt. Anfang 2021 erschien der Roman *Der Himmel ist ein kleiner Kreis* im Droschl Literaturverlag. Mit einem Ausschnitt daraus wurde sie zum Ingeborg Bachmann-Preis nominiert.

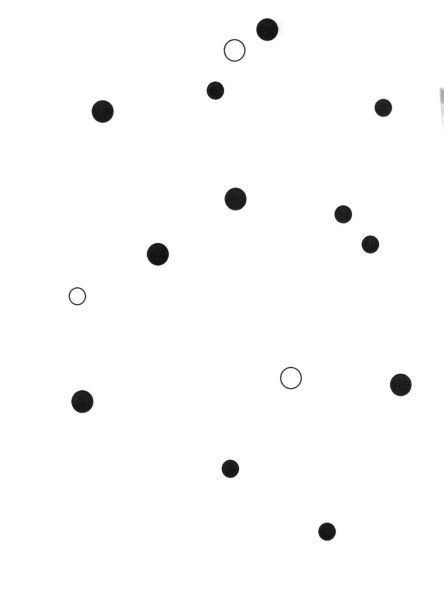